HOME SERIES

HOME SERIES
CHILDREN'S ROOMS

BETA-PLUS

CONTENTS

P. 4-5
Themenos designed this spacious room for a teenager. Custom-made parquet, desk and cupboard units in hand-brushed oak.

P. 6
Kenya (five and a half) in a room with furniture and fabrics by Flamant. The walls are in Tennis White paint by Flamant.

FOREWORD

P arents are often tempted to furnish children's room in the same style as the rest of the house. Other parents think that, as children grow up so quickly, there is little point in creating exciting rooms that will soon go out of fashion, so they choose a neutral and functional look instead.

However, this space deserves more attention. It is crucial to the child's development and wellbeing and should be based on his or her own tastes and temperament.

This is a room that contains a number of functions: a space for learning and playing, for sleeping and relaxing, and the place where children create their own fantasy worlds, their own territory, a refuge far away from the world of adults.

So it is essential to involve children in the design of their rooms, so that they feel a sense of ownership and enjoy spending time there.

This book presents a large number of children's rooms that achieve this aim of providing the perfect environment for the individual child.

P. 8
Twelve-year-old Joanne's room.
Francis Van Damme designed
the shelving to fill a wasted
space. Linen curtains by Libeco.

P. 10-11
A room for twins Théo and
Charles (one month old): a calm
and peaceful atmosphere. Cots
by J.S. Dreams. All accessories
are by Basile & Boniface.

A WARM, CONTEMPORARY

ATMOSPHERE

T he interior specialists from Sphere and Christel De Vos created several rooms in a beautiful country house, built by Vlassak-Verhulst, for a family with young children.

The look is warm and contemporary. A theme runs through the children's rooms: only one wall is painted, lending a modern touch and tempering the force of the chosen colours, thereby avoiding their typical associations. Red is not usually recommended for children's rooms, as it is seen as an aggressive, stimulating colour, but it is integrated beautifully into this room.

The TV corner of one of the rooms, simple and cosy.

The baby's room has softer colours and a calmer atmosphere, with a grey-green wall. The white wardrobe is by Flamant.

The same idea in this room: a single wall in sky blue. A Treca bed and Donaldson cushions.

A REAL REFUGE

A ntiques dealers Brigitte and Alain Garnier reserved the entire second floor of their beautiful country house for their children.

A timeless atmosphere in these rooms: natural shades for the walls, antiques, patinated furniture, romantic fabrics, oak floors. The neutral basis ensures that the decoration and furnishing can easily evolve over the years, as the children grow older.

A Canadian Adirondacks rocking chair beside a moose's head. The wooden floor is made of old cheese boards.

The boys' room. A Swedish chest of drawers between the two beds.

The girls' room.
The bed is in Ralph Lauren fabrics. Left, a wine table. Right, an old rustic table from Drenthe.

FIVE COLOURFUL ROOMS

The Sphere home-design store and Sphere Concepts interior design company, in collaboration with Scapa Home, created five children's rooms in a lively, colourful palette.

A consistent decorative theme in every room: a bright colour for the fabrics or walls, in contrast with the other walls, floors and white furniture.

The bed, the sofa, the Donaldson throw and the linen curtains are from Sphere.

La vie en rose in this little girl's room. A calm and gentle atmosphere.

Two children's rooms, designed by Scapa Home in vivid colours: a look that is more suitable for teenagers' rooms.

A harmony of white and turquoise in this children's room designed by Sphere Concepts.

IN THE FAR WEST

A Far West ambience in this fun room for a boy, designed by Cy Peys Partners. This is a very individual and distinctive room, which serves as a bedroom and playroom for the owners' eldest son.

Trendy shades (khaki, cowskin rug) in this unique space where the imagination can have free rein.

The walls are in pine panelling; the paint leaves the structure of the wood clearly visible. The tinted wooden floor is also in pine. A sofa with cosy cushions has been fitted into the slope of the roof, leaving plenty of space in the centre of the room, and containing a handy storage space.

Under the bed, a large drawer that can serve as a spare bed.

P. 24-25
A long view into the bedroom, as seen from the playroom. Custom-built wall panels separate the playroom from the sleeping area, reinforcing the sense of space and cohesion in this attic room. The dividing walls are in vertical planks, in contrast with the horizontality of the wall planks, which makes the room appear larger.

MAX, NOÉMIE AND EMMA:

LIVING IN THE COUNTRYSIDE

When they were barely four months old, twins Max and Noémie moved from a city home in Brussels to the countryside.

Their parents had the attic of their old farmhouse redesigned to accommodate bedrooms and a playroom for Max and Noémie (now six years old) and for Emma, the new arrival (11 months old).

The original elm-wood beams of the roof were retained and old oak railway-carriage planks were chosen for the floor. The rustic pine doors and fittings are based on antique models.

Emma's cot is by J.S. Dreams. The child's chair was found in an antique shop and upholstered in a Jane Churchill fabric. A custom-made Ebony carpet. A wooden floor in old railway-carriage planks.

An old pine wardrobe painted in white, by Baby & Co, with a curtain (fabric: Jane Churchill). Curtains in Egyptian cotton, with a thick lining to keep out the light.

A Flamant sofa.

An old deckchair for dolls, from Péristyle.

P. 28
Noémie's grandma sanded down and
painted her desk. Suede rucksack from
H&M.

Custom-built pine shelving unit by Grenier de la Chapelle.

P. 30
Six-year-old Max's room. The old bed from Baby & Co has been repainted and given a Lattoflex and a custom-made mattress. Sheets from The Conran Shop. Wicker basket and rug from Habitat.

A PARADISE FOR CHILDREN

IN SHADES OF WHITE

Pierre Hoet designed this house in a very streamlined and subdued style that is reminiscent of the magnificent country homes of Long Island.

The bedrooms of Kai (16), Ian (14), Indiana (7) and Kenya (5) are in monochrome white.

The combination of contemporary furniture (from InStore), old furniture and a predominantly white colour scheme create a very relaxing and harmonious look. These are bright and airy rooms.

An old bed and bedside table. The lamp is from Flamant Home Interiors; curtains from InStore. Kenya's mum has framed her pictures and displayed them on the wall.

A desk designed by Ann Demeulemeester, an Artemide lamp and a chair by Kartell, all from InStore. American blinds by Shabby Chic. American-style sash windows with curtains by InStore.

The doll's house is from Serneels.

A Shaker coat rack from InStore. A bleached oak floor.

An authentic Flamant interior,
with details including a desk,
a horse and a lamp.

A FAMILY OF KEEN COLLECTORS

A ntiques dealer Henri-Charles Hermans (Polyèdre) has three sons: Henri-John (12), Nelson (10) and Alexandre (5).

The boys' rooms are furnished in the kind of style that one might expect from this talented antiques dealer and decorator, with a great sense of taste and beautiful, timeworn furniture, charming objects and old pine floors.

Nelson in his attractive attic room. His parents carefully selected all of the antique pieces.

Nelson at work in his room. The floor is in reclaimed pine planks by Polyèdre.

P. 40-41
Henri-John's room. A wooden floor in reclaimed pine.
Henri-John loves to collect things. He has large collections of fish and antique glass and is passionate about miniature houses.

ALBANE'S ROOM

A lbane (4) lives with her parents and her brother Pierre in a beautiful villa on a leafy avenue in Brussels.

Albane's room is very British in style. The fabrics and designs in the room intensify the romantic atmosphere.

Nothing can be moved without Albane's permission. She spends hours in her room, drawing and making things.

P. 42-45
Albane's room. The white-painted desk, bedside table and chair are from a second-hand shop. Fabrics by Shabby Chic. White fitted units (p. 44-45) occupy the entire wall. Sheets by Shabby Chic and a throw by Donaldson.

ALEX AND IGOR:

GROWING UP AMONGST ANTIQUES

Three-year-old Alex's bedroom and playroom are up at the top of a tastefully restored farmhouse dating back to 1861. His little brother Igor (8 months) is a recent arrival to this charming space beneath the authentic oak beams.

Alex and Igor's parents love to visit antiques fairs and markets in search of original furniture and toys for their two sons. The result: a distinctive and very personal children's room, with a timeless atmosphere.

The white walls ensure that the pieces of furniture are shown to their best advantage.

Alex's bed dates from 1946. Alex's great-grandmother bought it for her second child and since then around a dozen children have slept in the bed. An Ikea duvet cover in red Vichy fabric.

The room is on the mezzanine. An oiled oak floor. The two Indian shutters conceal practical cupboards.

A farmhouse in painted wood (ca. 1940) and residents from Legoland.

A small, traditionally made bus in red and white painted wood.

P. 48

A strip of halogen lights illuminates the room.
Left, a pine chest of drawers from an ironmonger's shop: simple and practical for storing clothes for Alex and his little brother Igor.
On the chest of drawers, a basket with a willow handle and with a fabric in a bear design by Jane Churchill.

A DREAM BEDROOM

FOR LITTLE ARTHUR

S ophie de Kerchove is an interior designer. Before the family left Belgium to go and live in Tuscany, she created a charming room for her son Arthur (18 months old): a wonderful living environment, full of timeworn furniture, beautiful objects and subtle colours.

Soft beige and greige shades and a polished oak floor create a calming and restful atmosphere.

The wrought-iron bed is a family heirloom. The lamp is from a Spanish collection, with a linen shade by V. Pierre. The wallpaper is by Elitis, "Un amour d'enfant". Sophie de Kerchove selected soft shades between white and ecru, with a pale-blue quilt.

The old attic doors are in matte paint from the Ressource range of whites.
The wardrobe, designed by Sophie de Kerchove and built by her cabinetmaker, is in
a pale blue from the same collection.

A blind in a linen fabric from Baumann. The
white linen curtains are by Bruder (collection:
East End) and, like the blind, were made in
Sophie de Kerchove's studio. The designer
found the doll's house at a jumble sale.

As a child, Sophie de Kerchove slept in this wrought-iron bed. The red linen sheets are by Libeco. The quilted flowery cushion is from Mis en Demeure. The three poufs are by Marie's Corner. The bed canopy is by Colorique. A sisal carpet by Limited Edition. The mahogany lamp is by Bellino.

P. 52

The changing table is a design by Sophie de Kerchove. The baskets are from Habitat. Paint by Ressource. Mahogany frames around old engravings from a children's book. The lamp above the sink is by Aldo Bernardi.

The fitted units are in a matte paint by Ressource, with a patinated finish. Louisiana wallpaper by Nobilis.

LA VIE EN ROSE

EGLANTINE'S ROMANTIC ROOM

T en-year-old Eglantine has a beautiful playroom and a romantic bedroom in a country house with a beautiful view of the natural surroundings.

The playroom looks out onto the garden and is connected to the rear entrance, which leads to the garden. This allows Eglantine to run in and out of the house without going through the other rooms. She also has a view of the kitchen.

Brigitte Peten designed this sophisticated room. The bedroom is in beautiful, feminine fabrics, with old furniture and a few interesting objects creating an authentic and cosy atmosphere.

The playroom. The chair is from a flea market. The lamp is by Ellito. All of the curtains are by Ralph Lauren.

At the right height for playing: a pine serving table from antiques dealer Cathérine Berquin. Floor in Pietra Piasentina from Van Den Weghe.

Eglantine's Corolle doll is a fun playmate.

The fruitwood tables and chairs are from a local antiques shop. An oak floor.

The chest of drawers is a family heirloom. The standing lamp is from the shop A Room with a View.

P. 59-61
The wallpaper, denim fabric and striped under-curtain are by Ralph Lauren.
The bedspread and accessories are by Donaldson.

Eglantine's grandmother gave her this
chair. It is upholstered with the same
material as the Ralph Lauren curtains
and patterned fabrics by Jane Churchill.

A YOUNG, CONTEMPORARY

ATMOSPHERE

nterior architect Stéphanie Laporte designed this bathroom and bedroom for children in a 1930s home that was restored by the architects from The Office.

The two rooms have a contemporary atmosphere. The small bedroom is in white, with a few lively touches of colour: pistachio and fuchsia.

The bathroom has an illuminated ceiling. The floors and walls are in grey tiles. A Corian bathroom unit with an integrated washbasin.

Pale parquet for the children's room.

THREE TIMELESS

CHILDREN'S ROOMS

Interior specialist Brigitte Peten designed three children's rooms in this beautiful home, designed by architect Stéphane Boens and idyllically situated in beautiful green surroundings.

The three girls (Julie, 13, Laetitia, 12 and Aline, 9) have different personalities and Brigitte Peten ensured that each of the rooms was furnished with individual touches.

She selected luxurious and exclusive fabrics from a number of different collections by Ralph Lauren, Brunschwig and Pierre Frey, employing her sense of harmony and eye for detail.

Aline's room is decorated with Ralph Lauren wallpaper. Beds from Anker Bedding, in Brunschwig fabrics. The desk and chair are from a local antiques dealer.

A glass door separates the bedroom from the bathroom. Brunschwig curtains in thick felt, lined with a Pierre Frey fabric and with denim trimming. The chair is from Bruder and is upholstered in a Ralph Lauren fabric.

Inspirational architecture by Stéphane Boens, with a striking design.

A bed by Anker Bedding in a denim fabric by Ralph Lauren. The checked bedspread is also by Ralph Lauren.

P. 66
Wallpaper and curtains by Ralph Lauren in Laetitia's room. An Ellito lamp.

Julie's room. Ralph Lauren wallpaper.

A small sofa upholstered in a fabric by Bruder.

Curtains in Ralph Lauren fabrics.

Architect Stéphane Boens also designed the bathroom with an eye for detail.

CALM AND SIMPLE

T he bedrooms that architectural studio Themenos designs for its clients are often the most important rooms in the house: these are real oases of calm and cosiness.

This restful, well-structured room has a Long Island atmosphere and looks like a comfortable wooden cabin. The wood and the monochrome design create a simple, almost zen atmosphere.

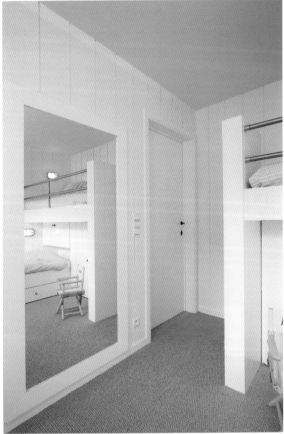

The wooden panels create a sweet effect in this room, designed for a child.
The painted finish brightens up the room.

GOING TO GRANDMA'S

F ive-year-old twins Louise and Charlotte often go for long visits to Grandma's house with their brother Jules (4).

Their grandmother has paid particular attention to creating beautiful rooms for her grandchildren. She has done all she can to create a second home for them. The rooms are tastefully designed with antique furniture and charming decoration: these classic and sophisticated rooms are all about romance and nostalgia.

Charlotte and Louise in a white-painted, foldable metal bed from the nineteenth century. The small cupboard on the wall is in mahogany and contains a collection of Charles X objects in palisander wood. Sanderson wallpaper.

P. 74
Louise on a chair that belonged to her great-grandfather. The corner cupboard is from antiques dealer Françoise De Vuyst. On the wall, a collection of English engravings.

NOSTALGIC CHARM

B asile & Boniface designed Noa, Sacha and Sidney's rooms, in collaboration with interior decorator Béatrice Bauwens.

Timeless charm, in a very English style, with a trend-resistant style for each child's room. The soft, pleasant atmosphere is reinforced by the pale pastel shades, the painted furniture and the flower designs of the fabrics.

Nine-year-old Sidney's room. The bed is by J.S. Dreams and has a built-in spare bed. The bedside table is by Sophie Décoration. The ceiling light is from antique shop Un Coin de Poésie.

Both units are by J.S. Dreams. Basile & Boniface can upholster the chair in a variety of materials (here, with a fabric by Elitis).

The desk and shelf unit are both from J.S. Dreams. Béatrice Bauwens provided harmonising touches in the carpet, colours and curtains.

P. 78
Six-year-old Noa's room has wallpaper by Special Delivery. The alcove bed with three drawers and the bedside table are by Sophie Décoration. The duvet cover is by Théophile & Patachou.

P. 80-81
Nine-year-old Sacha's room. A bed by Sophie Décoration. Left, a bedside table and lamp by Donaldson. Right, a small shelf unit by Ikea. A duvet cover by Everwood. The wallpaper with soldiers is by Imperial Country. The throw on the bed is by Designers Guild.

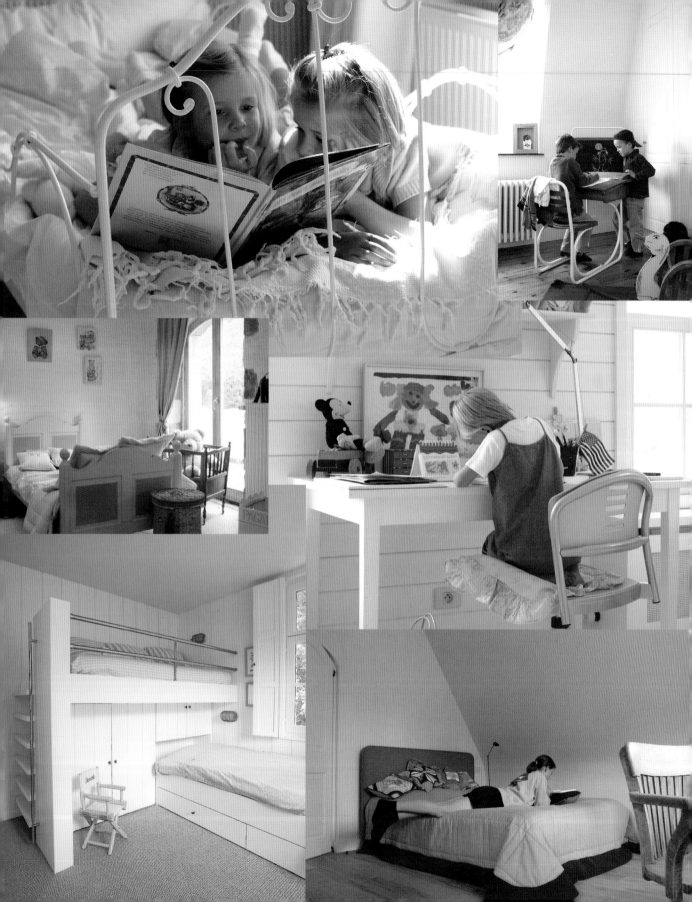

LIVELY AND INDIVIDUAL

S atchel (8), Sharon (7), Giorgio (3) and Jennifer (2) live in a tastefully furnished country home, idyllically situated in wooded surroundings beside a golf course.

Their mum took care of the furnishing and decoration of all of the rooms, paying careful attention to the character and interests of each of her children.

The whole project has a very lively and individual atmosphere: the ideal place for these growing children to relax, work and play. The decoration of each of the rooms is simple: no patterns on the walls or fabrics, but timeless elegance and soft, pale shades.

Seven-year-old Sharon's room. The bed and bedside table are from a local antiques dealer. Ilse De Meulemeester made the linen curtains. The lamp is by Donaldson. The pine planks have a pale-blue lazure finish.

Little Jennifer, in her big sister Sharon's room. The desk, chair and lamp are from College Kids.

The chest of drawers, the animal heads and the lamp are from College Kids. The bear is from Pepe Club.

P. 86
Three-year-old Giorgio's room. The bed is from College Kids and the chair is from Flamant. The wooden floor has a white lazure finish.

LÉO'S ROOM

L éo is only one month old, but he already has a fully furnished room, decorated with beautiful furniture and objects from flea markets and second-hand shops.

The Brussels store Tant qu'il y aura des anges restored the furniture and adapted it for use in this nursery. Natacha de Baré painted the walls and created the lively friezes.

The small desk was found at a flea market and, like the other furniture in the room, has been fully restored.

All of the furniture was painted in Lapland white oil paint, as the parents preferred to experiment with the colours of the walls. The fabric for the blinds came from KA International.

A HOME FOR JEREMY

Seven-month-old Jeremy's room was designed by Tant qu'il y aura des anges: the old, restored furniture and objects create a cosy, warm atmosphere, where the baby can feel at home.

The small bed is from a second-hand shop in Brussels and was completely restored by Tant qu'il y aura des anges. In consultation with the client, the same finish was used for all of the furniture in the room. The carpet and the mobile are from Basile & Boniface.

A small Breton chest of drawers with an added changing surface. The antique wall shelves are a decorative feature and provide space for neat storage of a number of objects. The changing cushion is from Basile & Boniface.

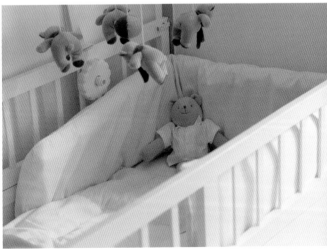

All of the accessories are from Basile & Boniface, except for the old toy chest.

BORIS AND ANTOINE'S ROOMS

IN AN OLD STABLE

Axelle Limauge, interior decorator and owner of Méridienne, a furniture and antiques shop, lives and works in the 17th-century stables of a historic abbey.

She restored the stables and lives there with her two sons Boris (10) and Antoine (7).

The rooms she created for the boys harmoniously combine modern and old elements.

The bed is based on a Provençal model and painted by hand.
Right, an antique oak cradle from Provence. Linen curtains and sheets from Libeco.

Antoine's room. Two old chairs repainted by hand. The pitch-pine wardrobe dates from the early twentieth century and comes from northern France. Axelle Limauge decorated all of the walls in Terre du Sud lime paints. Flamant carpet, Libeco curtains.

P. 94
Boris's room in the stables. An old
English bed in cherry wood. Sheets
from 120% Lin. Wall lighting by Hind
Rabii and a table lamp from Bellino.
The bedside tables are by Côté Table.

A PASSION FOR MICKEY

B ernard (11), Virginie (10) and Arno (9) have bedrooms that are strongly inspired by Donaldson's collector's items and furniture.

Architect Xavier Donck designed the house and served as interior advisor.

The three children each have a room that suits their character: tough and sporty for the boys and romantic for Virginie.

Virginie's room is very romantic and completely decorated in Donaldson.

The children's bathroom in this home designed by architect Xavier Donck.

Arno's room in white and blue. The beige fitted carpet in the children's rooms is very pleasant to walk on.

EMILIE AND PHILIPPINE'S ROOMS

Axelle François has two daughters, Emilie and Philippine.

Both daughters' rooms are tastefully furnished, with old furniture, hardwearing materials and decorative objects: classic rooms with a timeless charm.

In Emilie's room, a collection of old dolls, a bed from a second-hand shop and sheets and quilts from Axelle François's old shop.

The guestroom.

The desk is from a second-hand shop.
Colefax & Fowler wallpaper.

Philippine's room.
The armchair is from a second-hand market. The fitted wardrobe is an Axelle François design. Benjamin de Cloedt created the *trompe-l'œil* on the wall.

LONG LIVE COLOUR!

R Interieur designed these three children's rooms in very vivid colours. The hallmarks of this design are modern furniture and bright shades that are bursting with the joy of life.

Teen rooms in blocks of pink, bright green and orange.

BARBARA, VALENTINE

AND JULIEN'S ROOMS

U ntil recently, architect Bernard De Clerck, his wife and three children, Barbara, Valentine and Julien, lived in this distinctive Directoire house, which dates back to 1820.

He respected the structure and atmosphere of the Directoire house as far as possible, while decorating the interior in his signature style and colours and adapting the property to correspond to modern living requirements.

Bernard De Clerck's respect for authenticity, craftsmanship and fine materials can be seen in these children's rooms, with their timeless atmosphere and modest, unpretentious charm.

Twelve-year-old Barbara's room. Her bed is by Habitat, with a canopy from Baby & Co. The spread and valance are from the Malabar collection.

Bedclothes from the Malabar collection. The cupboards are made from old doors.

A refurbished Lloyd Loom desk chair. The nineteenth-century pine desk is from Finland. The pitch-pine floor is an original feature. On the walls, striped wallpaper by Laura Ashley.

A built-in washbasin in a cupboard made of old door panels. The mirror is from Carpe Diem.

P. 108
The bed canopy is from a second-hand market in Mézilles. The plaster bas-relief is a reproduction. Bedclothes from the Malabar collection.

A Directoire cabinet and an Anthracite lampshade (Natalie Haegeman). A 19th-century bistro table with a white marble top.

Laura Ashley wallpaper. A mahogany Empire chair. A late 19th-century dark-stained oak desk. Jute curtains by Bruder.

A father's day painting by Julien.

A *lit bateau* by Baby & Co. Laura Ashley wallpaper.

AN INSEPARABLE TRIO

E liott (six) and Charlie (four and a half) each had their own room to start with, but chose to sleep together in one room, which meant that one of the rooms could be turned into a playroom.

Baby Margaux (eighteen months) sleeps in her own room. The distinctive old furniture and objects give all of the rooms a warm and cosy atmosphere.

Charming old furniture and pieces in Margaux's room. Tant qu'il y aura des anges restored all of the furniture.

The playroom.

Eliott and Charlie develop their artistic skills on a desk and a blackboard, found in a second-hand shop and fully restored.

Shelves, bedside lamp and sheets by Ikea.

P. 114
Both knights look ready to launch an
attack on this bed in polished pine from
Pin, Blanc et Fantaisie. The paper
ceiling light is by Ikea.

SHABBY CHIC ROOMS

T he Chintz Shop is a well-known name when it comes to shabby chic interior design.

Amélie de Borchgrave's shop offers a very individual and original mix of products, including fabrics by Shabby Chic, Gustavian furniture, sofas with removable covers and bed linen.

In this report, the young interior designer shows one of the most beautiful children's rooms that she has created.

Children are always welcome in this home, with its large spaces and bright, airy rooms.

Five-year-old Mathilde's room. The white-painted wooden bed dates from around 1900. The old quilt is from England. Cushions in Shabby Chic fabrics. Above the bed, a modern painting.

The bed is in a fabric by Pierre Frey.

Mathilde is sitting on an old hobbyhorse from Sweden in Louis' room. Curtains in "cabana blue" fabrics by Shabby Chic.

P. 118
Curtains in "cluster pink" fabric by Shabby Chic. The old chair is in Shabby Chic "cherry bouquet". The large Barbie house is made of wood. On the floor, a Romanian carpet with a butterfly design.

Louis plays with a Brio train on a kelim.

Mathilde and Louis at their play table. The antique children's chairs date from around 1890.

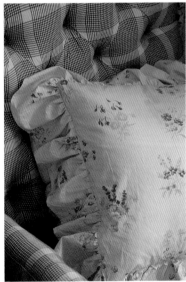

A cushion in an old fabric.

This painted cane seat is upholstered in Shabby Chic's "serenity blue" fabric.

P. 120
Louis' room: a big bed dating from around 1880. The quilted cover is based on an old design. The Shabby Chic cushions match the curtains. The rabbit cushions are made from strips of old fabric. A small antique chair from Sweden to help Louis climb into bed.

THE WORLD OF CHILDREN

F lamant Home Interiors is a well-known name in the field of interior design.

The company has always paid a lot of attention to the world of children and even has a Flamant Junior boutique.

The Flamant label can be found on beds, furniture, toys and decorative objects for children's bedrooms and playrooms.

A Tommy desk and an Anna bunk bed, both in antique white. A Corfu chair, Paresse white bed linen, a dressing gown from the Home collection, a shelf unit, Huggie Woolie bears and a horse with an antique finish. All from the Flamant collection.

Navy blue in this unusual bedroom. A mahogany sleigh bed, a Trevor canvas folding chair, a brown Clara wardrobe, wooden mini-consoles, a Navy mahogany desk, two coat racks with four hooks, a cushion and a linen bag from the Jeans World collection, bears and an Auster carpet.

Eliott (1) and Nanou (4) beside their Anna bunk bed. An antique-white Norfolk bedside table, also from the Flamant collection.

Ten-month-old twins Axelle and Julie's room.

Brown Clara wardrobe, single sleigh bed in mahogany, a linen bag from the Jeans World collection, a Julian bear (all from the Flamant collection).

 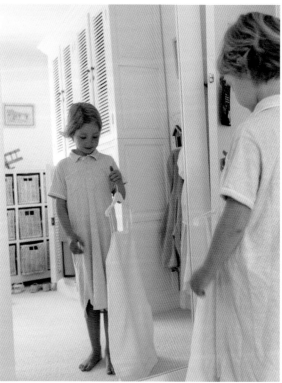

Five-year-old Aline's room: an antique single sleigh bed, an antique-white Norfolk bedside table, a lamp with a pink shade. All from the Flamant collection.